WARRIORS AND ANGELS

WARRIORS AND ANGELS

LIBERATING INNER POWER IN THE JOURNEY
OF LIFE

DR. SHELLEY MCINTOSH

J MERRILL

For permission requests, please contact the Permissions Coordinator at:

J Merrill Publishing, Inc.
2323 West 5th Avenue, Suite 120
Columbus, OH 43204
www.JMerrill.pub

Paperback ISBN-13: 978-1-961475-51-9
eBook ISBN-13: 978-1-961475-52-6

Book Title: Warriors and Angels: Liberating Inner Power in the Journey of Life
Author: Dr. Shelley McIntosh
Editing: Stephanie Newell

To Bessie Craig and Annie Miller—
I am your granddaughter. Your blood runs through my veins. I love you. I searched the census records for Escambia County in both Florida and Alabama.
To my great-grandmothers—I could not find you in the census, but I will keep searching. Based on the timeline, I believe you were both enslaved. I can only imagine how you lived. I honor you. I am your great-granddaughter. Because of your DNA, I live. I love you.
As tears fill my eyes, I feel deep gratitude for all my grandparents who came before me.

To my beloved parents, Rufus and Ruth Miller—
Thank you. I am proud to declare that I am the third daughter of Rufus and Ruth Miller. I honor you forever. I love you.

To my daughter and son, Lateefah and Italo—
You are my precious gifts! I am your mother. I love you.

To my grandchildren—Dwight Jr., David, Italo, Ni'Jah, and Saddiq—
You fill me with joy! I am your grandmother. I love you.

To my nieces, Joy and Jakneka, and nephews, Rufus III and Jovan—
Unbroken bonds are eternal. I am your aunt. I love you.

To my great-nieces, Jziah, Jade, and Jasir—

Beautiful young women, you made me a great-aunt. I love you.

To my sisters, Jackie and Vernice, and my brother, Rufus James Jr.—
Our shared experiences shaped me. I love you.

To my family and relatives across space and time—
Those who are still here and those who have disappeared—thank you. My
love is everlasting.

ACKNOWLEDGMENTS

Thank you to the publishing team at J Merrill Publishing—you have done it again. Guiding me through the publishing process has been a blessing.

CONTENTS

INTRODUCTION

Majestic trees stood with outstretched branches, yet bore no leaves—signaling that winter was arriving. On a chilly Sunday morning, my mother, Ruth Miller, entered Henry Ford Hospital in the heart of Detroit. I had been delicately forming in her womb.

My cells had divided and then united to shape my internal organs, each carrying messages from the Creator to determine my height, hair color and texture, skin tone, facial features, and gender. Within me pulsed the mitochondrial DNA of the first Black woman—the origin of all humankind.

For nine months, my mother internally incubated and nourished me. With the synchronous breath and rhythm of the universe, my mother and I sensed the time was near. As she contracted, I cooperated. On November 20, 1949, at 3:45 a.m., with one final push, the universe opened a space and welcomed my arrival into the light—all eight pounds and three ounces of me.

The same power that created me lived within me as cosmic energy and creative intelligence. I held the power to grow, create, and fulfill my potential. But how would that power be nurtured? How would it be revealed?

In traditional African society, the term *warrior* refers to a social group dedicated to military service. Warriors embody bravery, resilience, and protection—and are more than mere physical fighters. They also play vital roles in community defense, leadership, and cultural identity. *Angels,* on the other hand, are seen as guardians and protectors—intermediaries between the divine and the living, offering guidance and shielding from harm.

This is my story of warriors and angels.

For behold, the kingdom of God is within you.

— LUKE 17:21

1

EARLY YEARS

I was a quiet middle daughter. My mother said I was timid and shy, that I withdrew whenever she or my father raised their voices. So, they took a gentler, sympathetically stern approach —mostly by not hollering at me. In my sensitive state, I was still required to clean the bathroom (I hated that job), wash and iron clothes, wash dishes, and sweep and mop the floors.

I was about nine years old when I performed that dreadful chore of cleaning the bathroom. I shook too much Ajax into the sink. My mother told my father on me.

"Rufus, come see what this child has done."

"Oh, you mad, huh?" my father scolded.

Then, pulling his leather belt out of his pants loop by loop, he whipped me.

Later in life, I mentioned that moment to my mother.

"Shelley, did you notice what happened to that Ajax can the next time you used it?"

"No, I don't remember."

"Three of the six holes were taped. I did that so you would never get a whipping again for using too much Ajax."

And I never did.

My mother was only twenty-two years old, and my father twenty-nine, when they made that 750-mile trek from Alabama to Detroit with a one-year-old little girl—my older sister. They left their mothers and kinfolk behind to start a new and promising life up north.

They were serious about being parents. It was a partnership. They intentionally teamed up to provide for and protect me, my big sister Vernice (who was a year and a half older), my little sister Jackie (a year and one month younger), and my baby brother, Rufus James Jr., who was four years younger.

My mother was a stay-at-home mom for most of my childhood. She laughed a lot, taught us to play games, and made sure we took care of household chores. She sent her three girls to charm school, kept us clean and groomed, and maintained an orderly and neat home. My mother was friendly and generous, always helping others —sharing her cakes and sweet potato pies, caring for her sisters' children, and giving sugar and flour to neighbors—all done, as she said, "out of love."

My father, pastor and founder of Greater Love Missionary Baptist Church, told jokes he laughed at before anyone else did! He was committed to teaching us life skills. He taught me how to wash clothes, how to catch the bus and get a transfer. He gave lessons on how to add columns of numbers in my head, the importance of paying bills on time, and how to get a library card. He made us learn a new Bible verse every week, which we recited at each Sunday breakfast. He even taught me how to drive—and how to measure, cut, and install a rubber washer on a leaky faucet!

He studied the Bible, illustrators, and commentators to prepare his sermons. He took us to church every Sunday in snow, sunshine, or rain. In the winter, sidewalks on Vernor Street weren't shoveled. We had to walk thirteen blocks to the St. Jean bus stop from our house on Bewick. Lining his four children in single file, he took his place at the head of the line saying, "Walk in my footsteps." His size thirteen shoes became our shoveled path.

He also took us to the park on Fisher and Jefferson. He pushed us on swings, let us climb and hang from the monkey bars. We'd run wild in the joys of play and the ecstasy of nature. He'd walk us by the marina to gaze at the white boats bobbing on the shore of the Detroit River. That walk was magical—the final leg of our park adventure.

In 1965, when he could finally afford a car—a Fury III—he piled us in as we staked out our seats.

"I'm sitting in the back by the window."

"I got the other window in the back."

"I got the front seat."

That was three positions. The last one who didn't holler their claim in time always sat in the miserable middle back seat. After sitting there too many times, I had to perfect my timing. Before my father could even finish saying we were going for a ride, I'd quickly declare, "I have the front seat." Sometimes I won. Sometimes I didn't. But I always wanted to go for the ride—no matter where I sat.

My father always drove us outside our eastside neighborhood. Heading south on Bewick and turning east on Kercheval, we passed Garland, Fairview, St. Jean, and Conner. I gazed at the storefronts, watching people on the sidewalks. As we rode farther, the storefronts became more modern and colorful. The number of Black people faded like smoke until I saw them no more.

He drove slowly through the residential streets of Grosse Pointe. I could glimpse elaborate chandeliers, elegant furniture, and framed artwork through their unfortified windows. I often imagined how the people in those homes lived. What I saw clearly was a world outside of my own.

I didn't like to be threatened or mistreated. I remember being about nine years old when my mother left the house briefly, leaving my older sister, Vernice, in charge. She was only ten, but she took her role seriously.

"Sit down," she demanded.

"No," I responded angrily.

Suddenly, she found a belt and threatened to whip me. Oh no! Crying and retreating, I grabbed an empty box, threw my pajamas in it, and marched toward the door. I was running away!

But then I heard the key turn in the downstairs door—my mother was back. Thinking fast, I backtracked through the upstairs door, put the pajamas back in the drawer, and tossed the box aside. I couldn't let her know I was about to run away. I surely would've gotten a spanking. I reacted like a child—because I was a child. And getting in trouble with my mother was scarier than letting her know I was on the run.

I didn't tell on my sister. And that was the last time Vernice took her big sister role seriously enough to threaten me with a whipping.

I enjoyed challenges. They seemed like sweet peaches dangling from a tree—I only had to reach for one, pick it, and savor its taste. Succeeding was superbly satisfying.

We had a candy drive at Scripps Elementary School. The principal announced a contest for students to create posters for advertisement. The best poster would win. I worked on mine, carefully measuring and drawing orange boxes of candy with eyes, legs, arms, and talking bubbles that said, "Please buy me." I won! The sheer joy of being competent was more than enough for me as a fourth grader.

Acting—or not acting—on emotions was a difficult lesson. In the fifth grade, we square danced to the song "Bingo." In one stanza, we sang each letter: B-I-N-G-O, and Bingo was his name-O. As we spelled out each letter, we moved to another classmate. But when the final "O" was sung, that person became your dance partner. I would count the students and the letters, hoping not to end up with Joseph as mine. I dreaded dancing with Joseph because he was dark and had sweaty hands. Shame on me for the color discrimination—the sweaty hands, though, just turned my stomach. Yet, it seemed I had to dance with Joseph too many times.

One day at dismissal, my sister Jackie and I were crossing Kercheval, guided by the adult safety guard—a tall white man. With his red-and-white stop sign held toward traffic, he waved us forward. Just then, I noticed Joseph walking beside me. I don't know what came over me... a strange and mean spirit!

I tightly balled my fist and punched him in the jaw—for no

earthly reason! He didn't hit me back. My brief satisfaction vanished quickly. I had been trying to win the "Best Safety Girl" award by helping other students cross the street. I even practiced walking in the middle of the sidewalk, not near the curb, hoping the safety guard would notice how good I was.

Well! I didn't win. The same adult safety guard who had the power to choose saw me throw that punch. In a split second, I had destroyed my fifth-grade dream. A safety girl is supposed to protect, not attack.

Although quiet, I could be stubborn. I asked a lot of questions, especially when I wanted something. Back then, a whipping was a major method of discipline. It may have stemmed from the scripture "Spare the rod, spoil the child," or perhaps it was a remnant of slavery days. In my family, it was used to enforce obedience. When words failed to curb misbehavior, a whipping made it clear!

As I neared sixth-grade promotion, I was expecting a new dress.

"Momma, when are you going to buy my new dress?"

"You're not going to get one," she replied.

"But you bought Vernice one when she was promoted from the sixth grade," I said, disappointed and desperate.

"Shelley, you can wear Jackie's dress—the green and navy-blue plaid one with the white crisscross panels."

Okay, that battle was lost. I tried a new approach.

"Well, can I wear stockings? Vernice wore stockings."

"No. You're too young to wear stockings," she replied.

I was doubly disappointed. My momma didn't bend to any of my requests.

But Vernice quietly approached me when our mother wasn't looking.

"Shelley, don't worry," she reassured.

She handed me a pair of stockings and two garter belts, which I stuffed into my coat pocket. I left the house wearing white laced anklet socks, then stopped by my friend Francine's house on McClellan. There, I took off the little-girl socks and slipped on my big-girl stockings and garters.

I proudly boarded the school bus to A.L. Holmes, my legs wrapped in stockings like candy-cane stripes. At the promotion ceremony, seated in the first row of the auditorium, I wondered if anyone noticed all the raggedy runs. Suddenly, my name was called. As I stood, the garter belts inched down my skinny twelve-year-old thighs. Rolls of nylon bunched around my ankles. I awkwardly struggled to pull them up through the outside of my dress as I walked across the stage. Whew! I made it. My big-girl quest to wear stockings was victorious!

About two weeks later, Francine came to my house. While sitting in the kitchen laughing and chatting, she suddenly blurted out:

"Shelley, remember when you wore those stockings to school?" and laughed even louder.

My mother was in the kitchen. I could almost see her ears perk up like a puppy hearing a strange sound. I shot Francine a deadly look.

"What?" my mother asked. "Francine, you need to go home, because I promise you Shelley is about to get a whipping."

Francine left. My mother kept her promise. Her justification? I disobeyed.

None of this would have happened if Vernice hadn't given me those stockings and garters, I thought. But I dare not snitch on my sister. Secrecy was our silent code.

2

FOUNDATIONAL YEARS

*W*hen my two sisters and I entered our teenage years, my father explained, "Because you are girls, I may hurt you by whipping you on your legs and butt. I will not do that again. Instead, you will have to hold out your hand. If you drop your hand, you'll get another lick." We were being educated on the topic of a whipping—its history and its evolution!

The day finally came for me to taste the wrath of this new whipping. With my right arm stretched out and palm turned upward, my father hit it hard with a black leather belt. My right leg automatically kicked out. I stood there, sucking in each searing pain, determined not to shed a tear. After about eight licks, he was through. I ran to my bedroom, threw myself onto the bed, and cried —angry and in agony. Suddenly, I heard my mother's voice:

"Shelley, your father wants to know why you didn't cry."

With my face turned away, I answered, "Because I'll have to stand worse hardships in life than this." The response was spontaneous—I didn't really know what I was talking about! All I knew was that I shouldn't have to feel pain like that.

So, the next time I was about to receive a whipping, I strategized. As my father's belt slipped out of his pants loops, instant tears welled in my eyes. Moans whimpered from my mouth—cries loud enough to hear. If I started crying early, maybe he wouldn't give me as many licks. It kind of worked!

Although timid, I had the courage to speak up against injustice. My father told my mother that she could whip us—but never slap us in the face. He said his mother, my Grandma Annie, had done that to him, and he didn't want it to happen to his children.

One day, my brother just kept teasing and hitting me. His hits weren't hard, just annoyingly relentless. I called out to my mother three times to make Rufus James leave me alone. She didn't respond —just laid in bed like she didn't hear me.

I had just made toast sprinkled with sugar, cinnamon, and butter. My brother picked it up off the stove and smashed it into my freshly pressed hair, which now smelled like butter. That was it! I picked up a shoe and threw it at him. It landed right on the bridge of his nose. He fell to the floor, screaming and crying. At that moment, my mother jumped out of bed—she was a sudden blur coming at me.

Within seconds, I felt a painful, penetrating blow to my face. She slapped me!

Through the shock and tears, I remembered what my father had said. I couldn't wait until he came home from work. As soon as he walked through the door, I met him:

"Daddy, Momma slapped me today."

He didn't ask why or what I had done. He simply spoke loudly, but respectfully, while I stood there.

"Ruth, I told you not to slap these children."

The awareness didn't hit me then, but later I thought: I told on my mother! That was so bold. She didn't chastise me for it. All I knew was this—no one, not even my mother, was supposed to slap me. My father said so.

My momma still had her authority, though. When I was sixteen, she gave me my final and last whipping. I was simply sitting on the porch with my friend Dwight, who lived down the street. He was so handsome—brown-skinned, tall, slim, a small black mole above his lip, and had the coolest walk. I was beyond infatuated. While still talking with Dwight, my mother called out:

"Shelley, it's time to come upstairs."

We lived on the upper level of a duplex.

"Okay, Momma, just a minute," I responded sweetly.

"Just a minute, huh! Get a switch on the way up."

I thought, *She's not going to whip me for saying that... is she?* She had just embarrassed me in front of Dwight! He slowly stood and walked back down the street to his house. I, on the other hand, walked into the backyard to find a switch—a thin branch, mainly from a tree. I had to find one about two feet long. I searched the ground, found none, so I broke one off the peach tree.

Fear and tears welled up as I plucked off the leaves. To get a suitable switch was a perilous practice.

I didn't have the nerves my younger sister Jackie had. When she was told to get a switch, she'd stay outside as long as possible and return with the thinnest, shortest twig that could barely fit between two fingers.

But me? Oh no—I picked out a switch that met all the specifications. My mother hit me on my legs. I cried more from not understanding what I had done wrong. The next day, whip marks still visible, I had to go to my summer job as a playground supervisor. The uniform was a white shirt and navy-blue skirt. My strangely marked legs were in full view. I thought everyone could see those marks. Riding the Charlevoix bus, getting off on my street, walking past houses—I wondered if all the neighbors knew.

Maybe if I had said, *"Okay, Momma, I'm coming right up,"* I could have avoided the whipping. But I had said, *"Just a minute."* Even though I said it sweetly, my mother thought differently. I can only imagine her internal monologue:

"I am your mother. When I say it's time to come in, that means NOW!"

I wished I'd had the sense to anticipate a whipping. Sitting with Dwight for another minute wasn't worth it.

I made the honor roll every year from kindergarten through

twelfth grade. In elementary school, I became a safety girl. I was also a flag girl, responsible for raising the American flag on the school grounds. I lowered it after school, folded it properly, and placed it in its designated spot—only to do it all again the next day. Flag girls were rewarded with a hot cup of cocoa. I really enjoyed that simple treat!

Rosalind, Linda, and Carolyn were my best friends—a tight group of four in high school. All of us were smart. However, we were labeled as "squares" because we weren't fast girls. Popularity was never my goal, but I knew a lot of people, and a lot of people knew me.

High school was a joy! I attended all the dances, basketball games, football games, and track meets. With delight, I watched my classmates perform in spring plays and Christmas concerts. I even attended three proms. This time, my mother did buy me new dresses —and stockings that fit.

Through it all, my ambition to achieve accelerated. I was a member of the Student Council and the National Honor Society, Study Hall Captain, Vice President of my senior class, and one of the top ten students—academically—in Southeastern High School's graduating class of January 1968, out of 350 students.

Joy, justice, lessons, love, discipline, dignity, pain, pleasure, safety, security, wonder, whippings (four that I remember—definitely enough!), and wholehearted hugs were all part of my childhood journey. Above all, I was loved, nurtured, cared for, and protected by my parents—warriors in their own right.

3

UNSETTLING EVENTS

*B*etween the ages of fourteen and eighteen, I experienced unsettling, unexpected events that shocked me beyond understanding. The assassinations of four prominent figures riddled my mind with questions born of pain and confusion. Hanging on my parents' living room wall were three pictures: John F. Kennedy, Dr. Martin Luther King Jr., and a white Jesus painted in the likeness of Michelangelo's uncle.

John F. Kennedy was the thirty-fifth president of the United States, elected in November 1960. I was ten years old at the time—old enough to understand that he was our nation's leader. Though I didn't know much about him, he and his family were respected in my parents' home.

I had just turned fourteen when breaking news flashed across our black-and-white television: the president had been shot and killed in Dallas, Texas, while riding in a motorcade. It was November 22, 1963.

The news ricocheted through my thoughts, searching the folds of my brain for answers. Sadness soaked into my emotions like a sponge saturated with water. Hadn't I seen Jackie Kennedy on television and in newspaper articles? Hadn't I become familiar with their children,

Caroline and John Jr., through pictures in magazines? Why would someone kill the president? I had no answers.

Malcolm X was an activist—one of our leaders. He stood for freedom and power for Black people. It wasn't until years later that I read *The Autobiography of Malcolm X*, but I vividly remember February 21, 1965. He was shot to death while delivering a speech at the Audubon Ballroom in the Washington Heights neighborhood of Manhattan, New York City. His wife, Betty, was pregnant with twins.

Why would anyone shoot her husband? Why would anyone take the life of a man with four children and two more on the way? He was only thirty-nine years old! Why Malcolm X?

I was still in high school in 1967 when Black people—*my* people—rebelled. Tired of police killings. Tired of the Big Four police squad. Tired of packed housing projects. Tired of poverty. Tired of being abused and misused by an oppressive system. We were just *tired* of being tired.

Anger erupted. Black people fought back in the only way many knew how at that time. They set the city on fire, broke into stores, and took what they could carry. Detroit became a militarized zone. Schools shut down. Curfews were enforced. The Army and National Guard were stationed at my high school.

The rebellion was televised, but I saw its aftermath in person. Mack Street's business district, once bustling with crowds and lined with clothing stores, record shops, groceries, and medical offices—including the Black dentist who once extracted my tooth—was reduced to burnt shells of buildings, never rebuilt.

Amid the chaos, my father pulled a hidden firearm from its place. I hadn't known he had one. It was a German Luger. He pointed to a latch and said, "This is the safety." Then he showed me how to unlock it.

"Shelley, this gun will always be loaded. If anyone comes through that door, take the safety off—and start shooting."

That was my first lesson with a gun. My father believed the unsettling times called for it. The life I was living began to unfold more clearly before my eyes.

The ongoing civil rights struggle was also televised. Black people protested through peaceful marches and sit-ins against racial discrimination. We demanded equal access to education, fair wages, jobs, and housing. Though I didn't participate in the protests, I watched vicious dogs attack children. I saw powerful fire hoses knock grown men off their feet and pin teenagers against brick walls. I saw white policemen, armed with billy clubs, beat unarmed women. I cried. I asked, *Why is this happening?*

Then, five months after my eighteenth birthday, I got the news: Dr. Martin Luther King Jr., a leader of the civil rights movement, had been assassinated. It was April 4, 1968. He was shot on the balcony of the Lorraine Motel in Memphis, Tennessee, while supporting African American sanitation workers fighting for better working conditions and fair wages.

"Oh God." "Why?" "How?"

I was working at Michigan Bell on Van Dyke and Gratiot. My supervisor rushed in, saying the facility was closing and we needed to go home. Bewildered, I left the building and caught the Van Dyke bus to Vernor, then the Vernor bus to Bewick. I ran the rest of the way home. The fires in Detroit had already begun—and they were swift.

Once again, we were under curfew. Once again, the military occupied our city. I was stunned and heartbroken. Dr. Martin Luther King Jr. was gone—killed by an assassin's bullet. Why would someone shoot him? Didn't they know he had a wife, Coretta, and four children? Did they even care? He was only thirty-nine years old! It was too much for me.

Then, only two months later—on June 6, 1968—Robert F. Kennedy was assassinated. It was my father's forty-ninth birthday. Robert was the younger brother of President John F. Kennedy—a senator, a presidential candidate, and a civil rights advocate. While addressing supporters at the Ambassador Hotel in Los Angeles, he was gunned down.

At the time of his death, he had ten children. His wife, Ethel, was pregnant with their eleventh. Again, I asked: Why? Couldn't the shooter see he was a father? Didn't they care that his unborn child would never feel his touch or see his face? He was only forty-two years old.

My eighteen-year-old mind was reeling. In my short life span, four public figures had been assassinated. Thoughts raced. Questions darted in and out of my consciousness like flickering fireflies. *What kind of world is this? Do I even want to bring a baby into this society? What is really going on? Why won't someone explain it to me?*

Fear and pain struck me like a bolt of lightning. I had entered an era of questions—and ugly, stark realities.

4

CONTEMPLATING MY PATH

"Get your education, Shelley. That is one thing they can't take away from you." Those were my father's words—words that consciously and unconsciously motivated me to attend college, even though I didn't yet know who the "they" were. He trained me to be independent and confident.

My parents did not escort me to college. They didn't need to. I already knew how to enroll, what forms to complete, and which buses to catch.

Since I was a January graduate, I had time to work before the semester started. I worked at Peppy's fast food hamburger place, at Sears as an office worker, and at the Michigan Bell Company on the night shift in a factory. Though I only worked at Peppy's for about four weeks, I had no problem asking for a raise. I approached the supervisor and began my request.

"I would like to get a raise."

"Oh, you do? Well, work the north window and I'll see what you can do."

The north window was the busiest. I dove in like a whirlwind. With a pleasantly polite demeanor and a fabulously friendly voice, I greeted each customer.

"Good morning. May I help you?"

"I'd like two cheeseburgers and an order of French fries."

I moved like a shooting star—grabbing the burgers and fries, throwing them in a bag, ringing them up, collecting the money, giving change, and greeting the next customer. Order, bag, ring, change, repeat! I knew I was tearing that window up—so fast, so proficient, so polite.

After all that hard work, my shift finally ended. Proudly, I went to the supervisor.

"Well, do I get a raise?"

"You did very well. Yes, you deserve a raise. It will be five cents."

"What? Only five cents for all that work?"

"Yes. You'll now make $1.30 an hour."

I quit the next week.

Working at Sears and Michigan Bell was better—less physical labor, better pay.

I considered attending an out-of-state university, but I felt more comfortable staying in Detroit and living with my parents. I enrolled at Wayne State University with three of my friends and was accepted into the newly formed physical therapy program. Out of thirty students, only eight of us were Black.

My grades ranged from As to Bs, but a placement test was required for the math course. I took the test—and failed. I enrolled in a remedial math class, passed with a "P," then took the test again—and failed again.

Distraught, I was the last Black student to drop out of the physical therapy program.

Later, I discovered that the math class itself was easier than the test. I also learned that many white students had others take the test for them. These unauthorized test takers simply showed ID cards—no photo required—and went undetected. And just like that, they were on their way to becoming physical therapists.

Feeling defeated, I wondered: *How should I continue?*

I didn't share this dilemma with my parents. Instead, I shifted my focus to business courses, along with my remaining liberal arts requirements. One such class was sociology.

The professor was a medium-tall white man, about forty years old, with brown hair and an air of authority. Using the assigned textbook as justification, he declared that Black people were inferior.

A fiery sensation stirred deep in my soul. I had already read in that same textbook that babies in a village in Africa could recognize their mothers at two weeks old and walk at five months. There were even black-and-white photos of these children.

I raised my hand.

"On page 170, it states that these Black children are extraordinary, not inferior. Why did you say they were inferior?"

Caught off guard, the professor stumbled. He hadn't read ahead. Embarrassed, he tried to maintain his arrogant stance by dismissing the passage as insignificant and untrue.

It was in that moment that I began to see society more clearly.

Uncertain times continued to unfold between the ages of eighteen and twenty-one. The Vietnam War was in its thirteenth year. I knew of it only because young men from my neighborhood—and classmates—were being drafted.

Why is this war being fought?

Why are young men dying?

Why must they go to war when they don't want to?

Do they have a say in their lives?

The protests were growing. I needed to do my part. I marched with hundreds of Wayne State students. With signs and posters waving, we moved down Cass Avenue, then Woodward Avenue, into downtown Detroit, chanting:

"Hell no! We won't go!"

"Hell no! We won't go!"

That war didn't end until 1975. Some of the brothers I knew never came home. Those who did returned changed. Dwight—the one I got a whipping for—came back from Vietnam. But he wasn't the same. The shock of war cast a dark shadow over the neighborhood. It touched every family. We felt a collective sadness.

After three and a half years at Wayne State, I decided to quit.

Why am I wasting time when I could be making money?

Soon after, I was employed by the City of Detroit in the Labor Relations Department. When a new Labor Relations division was created for the Police Department, my young white boss and I were transferred to Police Headquarters at 1300 Beaubien. We worked out of a small office—pioneers in the department.

I came into my own identity during that time—a quiet militant who studied and read books by Black authors only. My rebellion surfaced in small acts: showing up late and ignoring the dress code. Foolish in hindsight, but it paved my road to suspension. I had no one to blame but myself.

I quit that job when, at twenty-one, I joined the Shrines of the Black Madonna. The next thirty years would become a socio-emotional, life-changing journey.

5

DISCOVERING BLACK CHRISTIAN NATIONALISM

By the age of twenty-one, my mind and soul were searching for deeper understanding. I had entered that stage where a unique movement of expanded inner energy takes hold—a time of growth, creativity, and purpose. The blossoming of these into full bloom can only be enhanced in a nurturing environment. For me, the Shrine of the Black Madonna was that place.

My sister Vernice—the same one I once fought over a worthless foam hair roller—became my guiding angel. She had bought *The Black Messiah*, written by Reverend Albert B. Cleage Jr., while shopping at the Shrine of the Black Madonna Bookstore and Cultural Center on Livernois. As she showed off her new earrings and bangles, she also pulled the book out of her bag. I quickly asked if I could read it. She agreed—but reminded me, as big sisters do, that it was hers.

I read it in three days.

"Vernice, let's go to that church."

"Okay! We'll go this Sunday," she replied happily.

We rode two buses to Linwood and Hogarth in the winter, with snow settled thick on sidewalks and streets. On the very first Sunday we visited, we joined. That moment—January 1971—marked the beginning of my journey as a Black Christian Nationalist.

Reading *The Black Messiah* was a revelation. The knowledge flowed through my mind like connecting dots in a drawing. When the lines between the dots are completed, a clear image begins to emerge. An apple. A flower. A bird. That's how it felt: pieces of understanding about my Blackness, religion, historical lies, assassinations, rebellions, wars, and theology began to converge.

WHAT?

"Jesus was a Black man?"

"He was also a revolutionary leader?"

"You mean Israel was a Black nation?"

"Romans oppressed the African Jews?"

"Jesus fought for freedom—just like Black people are fighting today?"

"Two thousand African Jews were crucified on the walls of Jerusalem the year Jesus, the Black Messiah, was born?"

"The prophets were all Black?"

WHAT?

Reverend Albert B. Cleage Jr. (Jaramogi Abebe Agyeman), founder of the Shrines of the Black Madonna, was the angel who set my world on an entirely new path. He had a crystal-clear understanding of the oppressive conditions faced by Black people and the systems that sustained them. His in-depth knowledge of the psychological damage caused by hundreds of years of brutal enslavement—and how that created a mindset of inferiority—opened my eyes.

I began to understand why my people acted in destructive or non-productive ways: they were responding to an enemy system they did not fully understand. The individualism, escapism, and materialism —I began to recognize those same behaviors in myself.

Reverend Cleage developed the teachings of Black Christian Nationalism and exhorted, "Nothing is more sacred than the liberation of Black people." To this cause, I dedicated my life. The knowledge I gained gave me meaning—it changed the direction of my life.

If Jesus gave his life for his people, then I had no problem being his disciple in today's world. I learned about our divine connection to Jesus, the Black Messiah. I embraced Black Christian Nationalism's *Teaches, Position, and Philosophy*—direct, concise statements that replaced everything I had previously learned. My mind was being renewed through disciplined, consistent study and training.

My new direction was environmentally reinforced. Reverend Cleage was intentional about transformation. This included changing our names. Mine became Monifa Dara Omowale, which means: *I have my luck, the beautiful one, daughter returned home.*

That new African name, coupled with a controlled, nurturing environment, was instrumental in changing our minds. Call and responses, revised gospel lyrics, and new songs were all designed to fan the flame of liberation.

Participating powerfully in the *Ritual for the Black Nation Call and Response*, I was drawn deeper into the vision and mission of Black Christian Nationalism. As I sang from the depths of my soul with hundreds of other young Black people, our voices rose like a cyclone —soaring upward, lifting the sanctuary roof off its hinges. We were united in purpose. United in power. United with the revolutionaries who came before us.

We identified with Jesus—the revolutionary Black Messiah— both historically and spiritually.

6

INVOLVEMENT WITH BLACK CHRISTIAN NATIONALISM

*N*ow, my path was clearer. My purpose was to free my people from oppression and exploitation, perpetrated by an enemy system fully clad in the sheep's clothing of white supremacy, yet suffused with the deceitful, wolf-like behaviors of discriminatory laws and policies—enforced and defended by the military and police. My resolve was sealed in the final paragraph of the Black Christian Nationalist Creed:

"I believe that both my survival and my salvation depend upon my willingness to reject individualism, and so I commit my life to the liberation struggle of Black people and accept the values, ethics, morals, and program of the Black Nation defined by that struggle and taught by the Black Christian Nationalist Movement."

This Creed bound me with hundreds of others who shared the same conviction. Together, we began to create a community, a sense of belonging rooted in collective purpose.

I was willingly assigned to a group of about fifteen twenty-year-olds. We understood our purpose. We held each other accountable to financial and recruitment goals, and we openly addressed counterproductive behaviors. Lateness, absences from group meetings, lack of participation in trainings, and failure to meet pledges were confronted—always with the intent to help each other change in service to our liberation. The group process was transformative.

When I became a group leader at twenty-two, I organized our accountability around protocol and norms. My group, Advanced Training Group Six, included an assistant group leader, Njeri, and three team leaders—Asim, Makini, and Kanye. Each team had approximately five members. This core drove our collective efforts. We gathered at my apartment's dining room table to discuss our plans and goals.

Each morning, I called Njeri. Together, we contacted the team leaders, who then called their team members.

"Good morning, Njeri. How are you? Today we're going downtown for *Kusanya Watu* (Swahili for recruitment), and we're assigned to clean the dining room."

"Okay, I'll make sure everyone gets downtown. We're working to reach our pledge—fifteen *malakeos* (visitors) at service this Sunday," she replied.

"Good! You call Asim, and I'll call the others."

This happened every day. Individuals made personal pledges, teams made collective ones, and the group as a whole set ambitious goals.

Reverend Cleage emphasized that salvation is a group experience. He introduced us to *encounters*—intensive group activities designed to heighten self-awareness and improve relationships. During one encounter, I began to recognize my defensiveness. I had used it as a shield, protecting myself from uncomfortable comments or criticisms. Once I saw it in myself, I saw it in others. I knew I didn't want to cling to individualism—it was a detriment to our survival. I truly wanted to change.

Consistent participation in group life taught me that transformation happens in community. The group process socialized us to shared norms and roles. It built cohesion and solidarity through persuasion, purpose, and leadership.

During one Christmas season, my group made a missionary

outreach pledge to collect $6,000. As Advanced Training Group Six —the "Six Machine"—we embraced the symbolic power of that number. As group leader, it was my job to secure grocery and department store locations (or "spots") where we could collect donations. I tried, but I failed.

At our next meeting, I confessed, "I couldn't get any spots, so we may not make our $6,000 pledge." Silence fell. Then, as if a stone had dropped from the sky, one member responded with clear disappointment, "But you said we could!" Another echoed the same words.

My group was not accepting failure. I felt the pressure—and I knew I had no choice but to deliver. I got back on the phone, calling store after store in different cities. Eventually, I secured the spots, and our group fulfilled our pledge.

The group process had changed me. Our minds became one focused force. Our actions aligned powerfully. Our behaviors evolved to reflect the values and ethics of the Black Nation.

I felt I belonged—truly belonged—with men and women who believed in the mission. And I began to understand how deeply a sense of belonging nurtures mental and physical well-being. It enhances self-worth, happiness, and resilience. It fosters acceptance, value, and support. Belonging boosts academic success, deepens relationships, and improves health. A lack of belonging, on the other hand, can lead to loneliness, depression, and despair.

Even when we hurt each other emotionally—through words or actions—participating in the group helped me recognize how I affected others. I became more aware of my behaviors and the need to consciously change them.

The intent of Black Christian Nationalism was to build that sense of belonging. But in order to do so, our way of life had to be institutionalized—something Reverend Cleage actively pursued. In 1972, he purchased the Abington Hotel at 700 Seward, renaming it the BCN National Training Center and Residence Hall. It became the heart of our communal living—a place for Black people to learn how to live together, depend on one another, and build a liberated future.

I was willing to move out of my home with my husband and into the BCN National Training Center. At least three hundred of us moved into the new building together. The nursery was established for early childhood care and social development. Mtoto House, the Children's Institution, opened on the seventh floor to nurture the physical, spiritual, social, and academic development of our children.

The Maccabees—the men and women of our security force—stood post twenty-four hours a day, seven days a week to protect both property and people. Office managers handled financial records and addressed residents' concerns. Cooks shopped and prepared meals in the communal dining hall. Assigned groups served food and cleaned the kitchen and dining area. The maintenance crew repaired light fixtures, patched walls, fixed floors, and solved plumbing problems.

All of this was accomplished by Black Christian Nationalists living under the same roof. We became deeply aware that we needed one another—and that fulfilling our responsibilities for the benefit of our brothers and sisters was a sacred act.

Group members were close by—next door, down the hall, one stairwell or elevator ride away. Naturally, we visited each other's apartments and shared our lives more fully. When someone fell ill, the group leader was there. When someone's heart was broken, a fellow member was nearby to console. When a young mother needed a babysitter, one was next door. When someone needed a meal, it was delivered by a sister or brother. I learned how to trust—and how to be trustworthy.

Something magical happens when a group moves in unison. Invisible bonds of energy connect us through tangible acts of love and reliability. Our lives became interwoven like links in a chain—strong, unbreakable—formed through the power of shared experience.

One day, Reverend Cleage asked me,

"Monifa, how is your group doing?"

"They are dependable," I answered.

"If they are dependable, then your group is doing well," he said with exuberance.

Filled with heartfelt joy, I added,

"I really love them."

This wasn't a selfish or ego-driven love. Words can't fully capture it, but I will try. It was a free-flowing current of joy—manifested through acts of respect, care, listening, support, and acceptance. Reverend Cleage called it *revolutionary love*—a transformative force, essential to our socialization and a prerequisite to the experience of God. He aligned it with the teaching of Jesus, the Black Messiah, found in John 4:20:

> *"If anyone says, 'I love God,' and hates his brother, he is a liar; for he who does not love his brother whom he has seen cannot love God whom he has not seen."*

I learned that love is a choice—not merely something we fall into. To love my brothers and sisters, despite our differences, was a choice that brought abundant joy. This revolutionary love created a bond, a sacred oneness, a unity that reminded us: we are brothers and sisters in the struggle. It called me to reflect before acting, to consider how my words and behavior affected others. It strengthened me to repair relationships through forgiveness. It helped us commit our lives to one another in service. And perhaps most powerfully, it laid the foundation for our shared liberation.

I understand that other groups—fraternities, sororities, churches, even gangs—may also feel a sense of belonging. But there were key distinctions in our belief system. First, we recognized the shared reality of Black oppression. Second, we understood our common history and common enemy. Third, we believed that individualism destroys relationships and threatens our collective survival. Fourth, we were convinced that African communalism was the will of God and grounded in the teachings of Jesus. Fifth, we believed that the Covenant—"I will be your God *if* you will be My people"—was made with a group, not with a single individual. And sixth, we believed that salvation is a group experience.

As a community, we sought the experience of God to empower us.

Using the word *we* created unity. That unity opened us to divine power. And that power strengthened us for our earthly battles— against everything that diminishes life, both individually and collectively. It propelled us to achieve what once seemed impossible.

I witnessed and participated in incredible accomplishments. We raised millions of dollars through grassroots collections in multiple cities. Members pledged and paid hundreds of thousands of dollars. We purchased properties in Detroit, Flint, Kalamazoo, Atlanta, and Houston. More than thirty of these buildings were transformed into churches, residence halls, nurseries, meditation centers, children's institutes, cultural centers, parks, and chapels. We bought 5,000 acres of land in South Carolina. It felt as though a divine whirlwind of power kept sweeping through us, pushing us forward to build and expand.

That power was healing. One of my group members was suffering from glaucoma. She came to me and asked, "Would you pray for me? My eye pressure is too high."

About seven of us gathered in a circle with her at the center. I placed my hands on her eyes as we prayed. "Almighty God of all creation," I began, "my sister seeks healing. I lift my voice to You— restore her eyes. Lower the pressure. In the name of Jesus, the Black Messiah, our healer."

A few days later, she returned with joy. Her eye pressure had normalized. "Thank you so much," she said, and we embraced.

Our unity created a community where I felt both physically and emotionally safe. Physical safety is the absence of harm. I lived in the church's residence halls for thirty-two years, overseen and protected by our security force, the Maccabees. Our community discouraged acts of aggression and actively shielded us from external threats.

But more than that, the community nurtured emotional safety— the sense of being accepted, of speaking freely, of being listened to, of being loved. It is the kind of safety where people set healthy boundaries, forgive one another, and grow together.

I would never claim that community-building was easy. We tried. We made mistakes. We tried again.

Reverend Cleage committed himself to the process of transformation—through group encounters, rigorous education, disciplined study, and spiritual practices like Tai Chi and Yoga. He engineered an environment where our behaviors could be reshaped in service to nation-building. More than that, he chose to embody that vision. He knew us—each of us—and he valued every life.

"We are saved many times." — Reverend Cleage

When I was about seven months pregnant with my son, I visited Houston, Texas, where his father, Italo Bugat, had been assigned. I was still living in Detroit, as the expansion cadre in Houston was too young to financially care for newborns. While there, I walked slowly down the median of Martin Luther King Boulevard. Later that day, I ran into Reverend Cleage.

"Monifa, why are you wobbling?" he asked.

"I feel a lot of pressure," I replied.

"If you feel pressure, you're dilating," he said, his concern evident.

"I'll see my doctor as soon as I get back to Detroit," I answered, my voice rising in panic.

I didn't want to have another baby early. My daughter Lateefah had been born five years earlier at just seven months, weighing only four pounds, four and a half ounces. I couldn't take her home until she reached five pounds. It took nearly three weeks. When the day finally came, I dressed her in a pink and white onesie, a crocheted pink hat, and a matching snowsuit. It was a chilly winter day, and she was wrapped snugly in a pink and white blanket. Sitting in the backseat, I cradled her in my arms as her father, David, drove us home.

As soon as I returned to Detroit, I saw my doctor. Sure enough, I was dilated one and a half centimeters. After an ultrasound confirmed the baby's size—and gender—I was given intravenous medication to increase my contractions. But after eight long hours, there was no progress.

As the medicine coursed through me, prayers poured out of me.

"Please, God, don't let me have this baby now. I've only gained ten pounds. My baby needs more weight. Please, God—hear my prayer. Stop these contractions."

For reasons the doctor couldn't explain, the medicine failed to work. He sent me home on complete bed rest.

I spent the next three weeks with my in-laws, Ernest and Willie Johnson. She fed me well. Every day was the same: eat, sleep, and sit on the porch. By the end of the three weeks, I'd gained thirteen more pounds. Confident that my baby had grown, I was overjoyed when my son, Italo, was born weighing five pounds and twelve ounces— enough to take him home with me.

The point is this: Reverend Cleage *saw* me. He noticed. He asked, "Why are you walking like that?" That moment reflected the deep care I came to know from him, both personally and vicariously.

Years later, while serving on the Bishops Council in Houston, a young man was brought before us for a disciplinary interview. He was behind on maintenance fees for the residence hall. One by one, each bishop questioned him, including me—with what I now recognize as an air of self-righteousness.

"How come you haven't paid?"

"When can you pay?"

"Don't you know it's your responsibility to pay on time?"

He answered quietly, "I just don't have it. I haven't been able to find a job."

Then, without warning, Reverend Cleage interrupted our questioning. Looking at the young man, he said,

"Your debt is forgiven."

The room fell silent. In that moment, I learned something powerful: true leadership requires understanding and compassion.

I observed Reverend Cleage facilitate encounters countless times. I listened to him preach and teach. Determined to be an effective leader, I embraced as many of his leadership qualities as I could.

In this kind of community, I thrived. As a full-time missionary, the church promised security—from cradle to grave. I had no rent to pay, no bills hanging over me. I wasn't in debt. I had a place to live and nutritious food to eat. My full responsibility was to contribute my time, energy, and skills to building a Black nation. And even more—my children were accepted as nation children. Dutiful adults helped care for and protect them. We built an environment where individuals could reach their full potential.

My journey began with the teachings of my parents. They took us to church, taught us Easter and Christmas poems, encouraged us to sing in the junior choir, serve as ushers, and lead Sunday School classes. They also made sure we learned practical life skills—how to wash clothes, iron, clean the house, and pay bills on time. Their love molded me.

My journey was further shaped by Reverend Cleage. Never in my young life could I have imagined the experiences and positions the Shrine of the Black Madonna would afford me.

Immediately after joining, I was assigned to an action group. I pledged and paid *Kodi*—a voluntary tax to help build a Black nation. I worked full-time then, and my pledge was $10 to *Kodi* and $10 to expansion each Sunday.

Kusanya Watu—bringing Black people together—was another responsibility. I passed out flyers and invited people to service. I performed every group assignment, including *Kazi*—communal work. I washed dishes, swept floors, cleaned bathrooms, and vacuumed the sanctuary. I was 21 years old.

Within a few months of joining, I was invited to a leadership meeting with about 25 group leaders and administrators. Part of our training included lectures and participation in the Sacrament of Commitment, facilitated through orientation—all required for new members.

During one meeting, the orientation director, Khufu, reported on how poorly the previous week's orientation had been managed.

"The red, black, and green candles were out of order," he said. "Wine was splattered on the trays. The African cloth on the altar was crooked."

I listened carefully and raised my hand. Reverend Cleage acknowledged me.

I said, "You can't assume everyone knows what to do. A checklist would help—review it with group leaders ahead of time."

"Make her a group leader," Reverend Cleage said.

That one statement launched me into leadership. At the young age of twenty-one, I was assigned as a group leader of fifteen peers—and I would go on to lead both adult and children's groups for over thirty years. Still in my twenties, I became a member of the National Coordinating Committee, the early leadership level of the Central Region at Shrine of the Black Madonna #1. I was later ordained as a minister, then bishop, and ultimately consecrated as a cardinal. Accepting assignments willingly became a badge of honor and a brooch of commitment cherished by every member.

I was assigned as the administrator at Shrine #2 on Detroit's east side and served as a member of the Houston expansion cadre. There, I developed and taught Black Christian Nationalism in Bible classes. I preached sermons, directed the Children's Institute (Mtoto House), created KUA small group devotionals, and served as a houseparent for children's groups. I participated in missionary and community outreach.

Each responsibility deepened my knowledge, sharpened my leadership skills, and enriched my relationship with God. Within the Shrine community, I reached my potential—and then continued growing to reach even more.

It was Reverend Cleage who urged me to return to college. After a seventeen-year hiatus, I applied to the University of Houston and was accepted. I earned a Bachelor's Degree in Interdisciplinary Studies with a teacher certification in elementary education. I went on to earn a Master's Degree in Curriculum and Instruction. Then, I applied for doctoral studies. My GPA was 3.9, high enough to qualify —but I needed to take the Graduate Management Admission Test (GMAT).

I chose the pen-and-paper version of the exam, but didn't score high enough. When I approached the professor overseeing the reading specialist track, he informed me that I hadn't met the gradient baseline.

Disheartened, I shared this news with the graduate office staff. Two African American women working there—angels, really—refused to let me quit.

"You better go back and take that test again," they said, sharp and insistent.

Their refusal to let me walk away reignited my determination. I took the computerized version next. But as the seconds blinked by in sharp green digits, anxiety took over. I couldn't even understand the questions. My score didn't improve.

Then another angel appeared—a fellow graduate student.

"Shelley, you can be sponsored by a professor. If you maintain a high GPA for one year, you'll be considered a doctoral student in good standing."

That was a miracle to me.

I reached out to Dr. Norwood, an African American professor who taught one of my curriculum and instruction courses.

"Dr. Norwood," I began, "I've taken the GMAT twice and didn't score high enough. Even if I took it again, I doubt I'd do any better. I heard that a student can be sponsored during their first year. Will you sponsor me?"

Without hesitation, he said, "Of course. I'll speak with Dr. Weber, the Chair of the College of Education. Wait in my office."

About thirty minutes later, Dr. Norwood returned.

"I asked Dr. Weber, and he said he remembered you—you've taken three of his research courses. Good news, Shelley: I'm your sponsor."

I maintained the required GPA that year and was officially recognized as a full doctoral student. Because of Dr. Norwood and Dr. Weber—two angels in academic robes—I was on my way to earning a doctorate in Curriculum and Instruction. That experience taught me that a standardized test does not define one's potential or future.

One day, as I walked the halls of the College of Education, I saw Dr. Nath—my former Social Studies Methods professor from my master's program. A tall, blonde-haired white woman with a professional bun, she was someone I admired for her creative approaches to teaching social studies.

"Shelley, have you thought about becoming a graduate assistant?" she asked.

"No," I replied quickly. "I'm in my first semester of doctoral studies taking nine hours. That's a full load—I don't think I can manage anything else."

"Slide an application under my office door anyway," she said.

Something about her presence made me trust her. Though I had no intention of pursuing the position, I followed her advice.

Within two weeks, she contacted me.

"I want you to be my graduate assistant, serving as assistant cluster coordinator for pre-service teachers. You'll work with three schools, each with three to five student teachers. You'll conduct pre-conferences to assist in lesson planning, observe instructional delivery, and conduct post-conferences for feedback."

I accepted the position.

Soon after, Dr. Nath left town. I coordinated with student teachers, scheduled meetings, traveled to each school, and fulfilled every duty. When she returned, she was impressed.

For the next three years, Dr. Nath ensured I had a graduate assistantship supporting pre-service and student teachers. She also served on my doctoral committee and—being an English major—generously edited my dissertation. She reminded me often, "You know your research. Don't let anyone intimidate you."

As my final dissertation defense approached, she asked me,

"Shelley, have you applied for a position at the University of Houston Downtown?"

"No," I replied. "I didn't see any openings."

"Submit an application anyway," she said without pause.

So, I did!

One month after I graduated, the chair of the Department of Urban Education, Dr. Bhattacharjee, called me. In her beautiful Venezuelan accent, she said, "Your application was the last one on my desk. There's no one else available to teach a graduate class for our very first master's cohort. Are you interested?"

"Yes," I replied. "When does the class start?"

"Monday," she said.

What? I thought. This is Friday.

"May I come to your office today?"

I quickly changed into a brown business suit and drove to the University of Houston–Downtown. During our meeting, I softly shed a few tears—my mother had recently been diagnosed with lung cancer. Still, I maintained my composure and asked about the professors who had taught the course previously and whether I could review their syllabi. Dr. Bhattacharjee explained that because of the short notice, I could simply discuss course expectations on the first day.

Her consideration touched me, but I knew these students—pursuing master's degrees—deserved more. So, all day Saturday and Sunday, I worked. I prepared a syllabus, created a PowerPoint presentation, developed student handouts, selected texts from my own library, and designed an instructor's format.

By Monday, I was ready to teach a three-hour graduate-level class.

That day, Dr. Bhattacharjee and two assistants came to observe. I was deep into the lesson; my students were engaged in discussion and actively learning. They were impressed. I had moved from being a visiting assistant professor to a tenure-track assistant professor, teaching at the university for several years.

My time as an assistant professor was demanding, challenging—and immensely rewarding. In the Department of Urban Education, I taught many aspiring teachers in courses such as *Culture of the Urban School*, *Social Studies Methods*, and *Educational Psychology*. I was also appointed Director of Field Services, serving as a liaison between the university and district superintendents to place teacher candidates in schools for student teaching.

My life was full—with the dual commitments of my academic career and my devotion to Black Christian Nationalism.

7

MY MOM AND DAD'S PASSING

*I*f I could turn back the hands of time, I could not—would not—ever believe that my experiences in the Shrine were a waste. Being involved in the liberation struggle helped place my life on the right path. I was part of a community that provided for and protected me, just like my father did. Where would I have ended up without the buffer of a sanctuary where I found purpose?

But I do have regrets—not because of the Shrine, but due to my own decisions. Serving in the expansion cadre in Houston required me to be separated from my parents and my fourteen-year-old daughter. They remained in Detroit while I immersed myself in nation building. My time and energy were consumed by teaching, leading groups, studying, attending meetings, facilitating KUA workshops, and doing outreach.

I missed my mother's birthdays, Mother's Day, and Christmas. One day she said, "Shelley, I'm embarrassed to invite anyone over because of the furniture." It was old and shabby. She rarely complained, but that stayed with me. When she turned seventy-six on March 8, 2002, I decided to surprise her. I saved money from my graduate assistantship and ordered a sofa, love seat, coffee table, end tables, and lamps.

When my husband and I visited her in Detroit, I gave her three birthday cards, saving the third one for last. It contained the receipt and delivery date.

"Shelley, what is this?" she asked.

"Momma, that's a receipt. You have some new furniture coming."

"Thank you, Shelley and Neal. No one has ever done this for me before."

She called my husband Neal instead of Awznee. He smiled and said, "She did that by herself."

The furniture arrived a few days later. My mother was so happy.

She didn't talk much about her health. I found out more when she visited Houston two months later to celebrate my graduation. She shed tears of joy when I walked across the stage and was hooded as Doctor Shelley McIntosh.

I always felt I would be the daughter to care for her. I dreamed of taking her to Hawaii. I didn't expect she'd be diagnosed with lung cancer during her visit.

"I'm so sorry, Momma. I just didn't know."

After radiation treatments at M.D. Anderson, she passed away on September 16, 2002. She never made it back to Detroit. She had planned to go to Chicago first to help her niece Cathy with a newborn. She told me,

"Shelley, do you know why I'm going to Chicago when I leave here?"

"Why, Momma?"

She spelled it out: L-O-V-E.

"Love," she said. "I'm going because of love."

Her death weakened my knees. I could barely stand. The pain swept my breath away like a river in flood. Losing my loving mother left me in a state beyond words. I still can't describe it. I just feel it.

My father lived in Pensacola, Florida with his second wife. A few months before my graduation, my husband and I visited. He was unusually quiet. While his wife was in the kitchen, he said,

"Shelley, come here. I want you to write this down. I want

Reverend Brown to preach my eulogy, and I want to be buried in Barrancas National Cemetery."

He had served in World War II and earned the rank of sergeant.

When I told his wife, she was surprised. "Oh, he does? I already bought two burial plots side by side."

"He told me what he wanted," I replied. "Will you respect his wishes?"

"Yes, I will."

"Thank you."

My father died on September 17, 2002—a day after my mother. His wishes were honored. The bugle played "Taps." A rifle salute was fired. The flag was folded and presented to his wife.

This grief was different. My father had been my protector and provider in life; I believed he would continue in death. Still, I was devastated, drowning in sorrow. I kept teaching my university courses, even with a dark cloud hanging over me. Tears fell while walking, driving, at night, during the day—spontaneously, unexpectedly.

My strength only returned when God spoke to me:

"Monifa, you had them both for fifty-two years. They have always belonged to me."

8

PARENTING REGRETS

*S*ome people say that they have no regrets in their lives. That is not true for me. When I was asked to relocate to the Houston Shrine from the Detroit one, my daughter, then fourteen years old, did not want to go back to Houston. I, with motherly authority, told her that she was. Her response: "If I do, I'm going to run away." Then, my mother authority rose to another unsuspected level. "If you do, I will chase you all over the United States," followed by a few licks on her behind. I was torn. My emotions stirred and swirled within me. I spoke to Reverend Cleage about my dilemma. He said, "If you make her go, she will rebel against you."

I prayed that night. I trusted the structure of the Mtoto House in Detroit and a close friend to take care of my daughter while I was fulfilling my assignment in Houston. I seriously thought and believed that I was building a better world for my child—a world of stability, of love, of institutions, of abundance, of Black power.

So, I accepted the assignment believing that she would be supported. My trusted friend did look out for her, but it was her father, David Scott, who took total responsibility. He moved her out of the Mtoto House to live with him and her bonus mother, Mildred

Scott. They raised her for the fourteen years that I was in Houston. I am beyond grateful and appreciative of these two angels.

I didn't experience my daughter Lateefah's high school days. David and Mil afforded her opportunities that I was unable to give her being a full-time missionary. Her father enrolled her in the best schools, purchased her first car, and supported her college journey. I believed that I was building a better world for her, that she would inherit the institutions I helped build, that she would be free, secure, and safe.

But I failed to face the reality that freedom wasn't coming that soon or that the Shrine would eventually travel a different road. My daughter felt that I put the Shrine before her. In other words, the church was more important to me than she was. That left a gaping, guilty hole in my heart—a piercing pain in my soul.

I always loved my daughter ever since I felt the little flutter of life in my womb when I was just three months pregnant. In an attempt to reassure her, I wrote a long letter to explain the rationale of my decisions. I wanted her to know that she was always loved.

One year we visited relatives in Chicago. Teef must have been in her early twenties. On our way back to Detroit, we listened to the song, "Zoom, I Like to Fly Away," by the Commodores. I love that song, especially the instrumental piece. I started a conversation about the letter I had written to her. It opened the floodgates of emotions—cascading with a child's anger even though she was now an adult, twisting like a tsunami with a mother's regret. We both shed tears laden with streams of anger and rivers of remorse.

"Teef, I am so sorry," I found myself saying more than once.

"Mom, we talked about that before. It's water under the bridge. Both my brother and I are okay. We are not in jail. We are not on drugs. It's okay."

At times, I am still laden with guilt and tears. If there was anything I could do over, it would have been to stay in Detroit with my daughter.

Time passes. Her father and I agreed that we both had her for fourteen years each and that it all worked out.

My son, Italo, stayed with me through his childhood and teenage years. We resided in Houston in the Shrine's residence hall. As a young boy, he was interested in looking at bugs—like a little scientist. Shortly after he graduated from Furr High School, he wanted to move to Atlanta where Shrine 9 is located.

"Momma, I want to move to Atlanta and enroll in a college. I may fall on my face but it's something I want to do."

"Son, if you fall on your face, you just get right back up and start walking again," I told him.

He did move into the residence hall in Atlanta. Then he moved in with a friend. One day, I got a phone call from his friend saying that my son had been shot and was in the hospital. Because I was on the communal budget, I didn't have much money. So, I pawned my high school class ring. I tried to pawn some silver platters but found out that they were just silver-plated. With monetary support from the church, I flew into Alabama, drove a rental car to Atlanta with only one compelling thought: "I am going to get my son."

Upon arriving at the hospital, I was relieved that it was a flesh wound, but I emphatically told him, "You are going back to Houston with me. That's final."

I seemed to always fall into the mode of decision-making and not fully embracing the fear or acknowledging the trauma my son had experienced. Being headstrong about saving his life, I failed to fully understand his interests, his aspirations. For that, I am sorry. He is now a hard-working father with a keen sense of humor.

I feel blessed that I have lived to see both of my children grow into adults and parents.

As I think about my children, I realized that I was a possessive mother. I am the one who carried them in my womb. I am the one who was in labor. I have first rights to them. What I failed to realize at that time was that they were the seeds of both me and their fathers, who loved them as much as I did.

With this aching awakening, I felt a need to apologize because it was I who separated them. I had moved to Houston as a member of the expansion cadre while their fathers stayed in Detroit. This awakening pressed hard against my conscience.

I called their fathers.

"I am sorry for separating our child from you. I am asking for your forgiveness."

I was forgiven.

Acknowledging that I did not think about how they felt or the pain that I caused was painful for me. I did not like what I saw in myself.

Both are good and intelligent men. Marriage didn't work out for us. But what worked is that we created new life—our children. They, in turn, created new lives and made us grandparents to Dwight Jr., Italo, David, and Ni'jah. In heart and practice, we are all family. We gather at Thanksgiving, Christmas, birthdays, and Mother's Day. Now, I know when I sincerely want to resolve past relational mistakes, I accept responsibility for what I did. Then the door of my heart opens, and I walk through. My soul is restored, and I am born anew.

9

MY RELATIONSHIP WITH BLACK CHRISTIAN NATIONALISM AFTER REVEREND CLEAGE'S PASSING

I wish that I had more foresight. When joining a movement, I should have considered a time when our founder, Reverend Albert Cleage, would be gone. After his death in 2000, almost everything I had experienced for thirty years changed. There were no more red and black uniforms, no need for African names, and no recitation of the Black Christian Nationalist Creed. The majority—about 25—of the church's properties and institutions in Detroit, Atlanta, and Houston were sold. It was stated that we were no longer oppressed.

My concern was that if the church—the movement—was taking a new direction, leadership had a responsibility to educate the congregation. Why? Because we deserved to know. I asked questions. I also typed up an analysis identifying problems and possible resolutions, hoping to clear up areas of confusion. I submitted it to the governing council but received no response.

After earning my doctorate and being employed by the University of Houston, I was willing to tithe a tenth of my monthly gross income to financially support full-time missionaries. I believed it was a progressive idea, especially since I had been one for many years. This would allow me to make a worthy contribution. I also believed it could provide a new avenue for others to do the same. I submitted this idea—no response.

The church had a ten-year expansion projection developed by Reverend Cleage. By his passing in 2000, three regions had been established: the Central Region headquartered in Detroit, the Southern Region in Atlanta, and the Southwest Region in Houston. After his death, a provocative message echoed throughout the congregation. It was even stated from the pulpit that older members stood in the way of progress. They were referring to the twenty-year-olds who had joined in the seventies—the ones who had sacrificed their entire young lives.

Upon hearing this, I spoke to the new leader:

"If we are being perceived as hindering the church's progress, form three expansion cadres. The ten-year projection includes New York, Kansas, and California. Each cadre can be sent to a city. Support them financially for one year while they establish themselves and pursue employment. This is a way that we can spread Black Christian Nationalism even more."

No response.

I felt that I no longer fit into the church or movement that I had helped build. It was very difficult for me to participate in something I no longer trusted. So, I shifted my time and effort to my work as a professor. Later, I returned to Detroit and became an elementary school principal. Because I no longer felt connected to the church, I stopped attending Shrine worship services. Instead, I went to church with my daughter and grandson, using the opportunity to spend more time with them and help make up for the lost years.

One Sunday, while at home, I was caught completely off guard when my niece, Joy, called to inform me that I had been excommunicated. Those words pierced my soul like a dagger. I had received no prior hearing or notice. The information was in the church's Sunday bulletin.

My Response – Letter to the Leader

By no means is this letter a request to re-establish membership in the Pan African Orthodox Christian Church. Rather, I have written it to express what I have heard and to state what is true.

I am accused of carrying out a phone and e-mail campaign and heading up an opposition group. This is not true. These are not my practices. I presented my concerns in discussions with you, the assembly in Houston, and through written memos.

Any issue that concerned me was discussed with you and submitted in writing to the Assembly of Cardinals. I believed that presenting my concerns to you—through the last memo I had written—would have been taken as something worth discussing, especially since I had been a full-participating member for 30 years. However, that memo was also viewed as subversive and unsupportive. I did share my concerns with those close to me, and I listened to other members' opinions—not to destroy but to help the church in the best way I knew how. That is true!

With that said, I forgive you and those responsible for my and my son's expulsion. As Jesus said, "Forgive them, for they know not what they do." There is no reason for you or security to investigate my son or me or to spread any more rumors. You will not find anything other than what you have already heard verbally from me. I chose to write at this time and not before because I had to digest these events. For me, it is the only way to start a new year. I wish always that Black Christian Nationalism lives, and I wish the same for the church. It will definitely live through everything I do. I do not expect any response to my letter as this serves to be my first and last one regarding this situation.

– Dr. Shelley "Monifa" McIntosh

"Dear God, please take care of me all the days of my life. You know my heart," was my prayer.

I, like many of my brothers and sisters, sacrificed with blood, sweat, and tears to build institutions while holding fast to that dream of freedom. What do we have to show for it now?

Sometimes I asked myself: Was my life lived in vain? Was my commitment to the church respected? Did anyone know the magnitude—or even care—about the work I had done?

I have learned that each person, including myself, who sees himself or herself as a leader of any organization—be it Black churches, fraternities, sororities, block clubs, or community centers— must be courageous enough to admit their own weaknesses and recognize their strengths. Then, be brave enough to re-evaluate, reset, and reform their ways to best serve the needs of our people. It is the divine duty of each person to raise their voice and to hold accountable those who choose to lead. This I believe. This I know.

For the majority of my years in the Shrines of the Black Madonna, I worked with youth ranging from two to eighteen years old. I served as the Mtoto House Director for over two decades. Mtoto House was the Children's Institution initiated by Reverend Cleage to meet the social, academic, physical, and spiritual needs of our children. Upon asking any adult why we were building a nation, the collective response was the same:

"We are doing this for our children."

10

REFLECTIONS

Over the past twenty years, I have deepened my understanding of my creation and the inner power endowed to me at birth. This power—the God within—has revealed itself in countless ways. Some moments remain especially vivid.

One of them is my 60th birthday. I decided to celebrate by throwing myself a party with the theme "Sensational Sixty." My daughter helped by recommending a couple of event planners. The venue, Burton Manor, was elegant. The DJ kept the music flowing, and the food was a hit. But the cake was a major disappointment—a small, two-layered thing with sparse decoration. It looked like it belonged to no occasion at all and certainly didn't satisfy any sweet tooth.

Still, the evening was unforgettable. A table displayed books and articles I had written, and a TV monitor cycled through photos of my life—my children, siblings, nieces, colleagues, and members of the Shrine of the Black Madonna. I had lived six decades, three full scores, and I was grateful.

My siblings came. My Aunt Rose, the youngest of my mother's sisters, arrived in a wheelchair. In her youth, she had loved to dance —and she was good at it. Holding both of her hands while she remained seated, we rocked together to the music. She was my last living aunt, and that moment stays with me.

Now, five years into my seventies, I reflect on where I am. I remain active as the founder and CEO of Child Focused Consulting Company, LLC. For over fifteen years, our company has provided professional development for teachers, Direct Instruction training, small-group reading interventions, private tutoring, and instructional coaching.

I am deeply blessed to work with a committed team of retired educators, most of whom dedicated 30 years to the Detroit Public Schools and have remained with my company for a decade. Their ages range from fifty to seventy-five. Their names deserve to be honored: Rosalind Gentry, Brenda Kokumo, Ula Barber, Kathy Gray, Dr. Barbara Williams, Arlene Rosemond-Scruggs, Rosalind Talley, and Michelle Owens.

Our shared vision is simple but urgent: a society where every child is afforded their civil right to become highly proficient in reading and comprehension.

I handle the preliminary work—submitting proposals, negotiating contracts, ensuring everyone on the team is signed on officially. I also require that we show up not only professionally but emotionally intelligent in our work with children. We participate in ongoing training in Reading Mastery, Language for Learning, and Corrective Reading.

Maintaining a cohesive team requires my full presence. I regularly visit each member in their school setting—sometimes to observe, sometimes to model instruction, and often just to ask, "Do you need anything?" I make sure materials arrive on time, knowing that their success hinges on my reliability, and that their efforts, in turn, spark the reading success of many students.

I am meticulous about paying them promptly. I don't ever want them to wonder when they'll be compensated. I send texts letting them know checks are in the mail—or hand-deliver them to schools or meeting places, always with a personal note of thanks.

When we complete a contract with a school, I treat the team to brunch or dinner. Each holiday season, I organize an appreciation gathering. We've dined at Eddie Merlot's, Eddie V's, Flemings, Petit Déjeuner, and P.F. Chang's. I gift them with flowers, bangles, movie passes, or massage gift cards. What began as my gesture of appreciation has evolved into mutual giving. At our gatherings, each person leaves with an armful of gifts.

I love and respect them. Some of us have known each other since middle school. We've grown into grandmothers together. We need each other—and that shared purpose, that sense of community, is why we've stayed committed to ensuring every child learns to read.

During the global pandemic, I shouldered the care of my oldest sister, Vernice. It was my greatest challenge. I made sure she had food, clothing, and medical care—picking up Meals on Wheels, ordering from Kroger, delivering meals, managing her bills, contacting her doctors. My mantra became, "Vernice ain't heavy—she's my sister."

But I was overwhelmed. One day, while driving the 24 miles from my condo to her nursing home, I broke down sobbing. On St. Paul Street, with tears pouring and hands gripping the wheel, I cried out, "This is hard! This feels so burdensome. But Vernice needs me."

Then I prayed, "Oh God, make me a cheerful giver."

We survived the pandemic—but our victory was brief. Vernice died suddenly in 2021. The loss shook me to my core. It was a different kind of pain, hard to explain. Marion, my dearest friend, said it best: "It felt chopped from the top."

On any given morning, the sharp, annoying buzz of my cell phone alarm blares—pauses—then blares again. Reaching toward the lampstand, I notice the phone's face flickering with white floating dots. I wonder why. Without an answer, I swipe the icon to the right. Silence. A small, needed relief from a necessary nuisance.

This morning, I lay still in my dark cherry wood queen-sized bed, cocooned in quiet solitude. A kaleidoscope of colorful memories gently flows through my mind. The Egyptian vanilla comforter I ordered online during the 2020 pandemic hugs my body. Stuffed with fluffy down feathers, it traps warmth against the chill—60 degrees inside, 10 degrees outside. Only my head remains uncovered, exposed for breath and ease. My eyes drift, taking in the space I've carefully shaped, the sanctuary I've made.

The bedroom walls are painted a soft pastel gold. To the right, three framed degrees from the University of Houston hang in a proud vertical line: my Bachelor of Science from 1996, a Master of Art in Teaching from 1998, and my terminal Doctorate in Curriculum and Instruction from 2002.

I returned to college at 42 with one unwavering goal: to finish. Five years for the first degree, two for the second, and three for the final one. When I was hooded as Doctor Shelley McIntosh at age 52, I wept with gratitude. Those degrees are not just paper; they are symbols of my tenacity—my refusal to quit.

Each morning in this sacred sphere, I remember the time I've spent on Earth and the many roles I've embodied: daughter, mother, grandmother, wife, widow, sister, aunt, great-aunt, sister-in-law, mother-in-law, cousin, friend, teacher, professor, principal, coach, minister, youth director, yoga instructor, business owner, author, activist, and a Black Christian Nationalist. My ancestral DNA reveals that I am Mende of Sierra Leone. When I learned that, I cried tears of joy. The circle had closed. I am many blossoms from a single flower.

My bed now serves a different purpose—prayer and meditation. I sit up slowly, arranging satin-draped pillows against the curved headboard, straightening my back. I no longer envision the traditional white Jesus when I pray. Instead, I focus on the dark expanse, the energy that surrounds me—God as omnipresent and infinite.

The teachings of Jesus, the Black Messiah, echo in my mind: "Ask, and it shall be given. Knock, and the doors shall be opened."

I speak into the silence: "This is a new day that I have never seen before. Thank you! It is the best day of my life, and I do expect miracles."

One by one, I envision my daughter, my son, my sister, nieces, nephews, grandsons, and my business team. I send light into their bodies—to bless, heal, and preserve them. Then I sweep the light through my own body, commanding it to vibrate with 100% health: heart, blood pressure, cholesterol. I whisper inward: "I will take care of you. Please take care of me."

Finally, I extend that light to the world. "Let corrupt governments crumble, and righteous ones rise. Let African leaders unite in sovereignty and righteousness for our Motherland and all African people."

Each day, I recite Psalm 23. Then I follow with affirmations:

"I am light, life, love, and power. I use my power for good."

"I let go of anger, worry, fear, and self. I'm thankful, kind, and a smart worker."

"I am young, vibrant, happy, healthy, wealthy, and wise."

I set a timer for ten minutes. Eyes closed, I listen to my breath—inhale, exhale. I follow its journey into my lungs and out into the atmosphere, merging with the divine. When the timer buzzes, I conclude: "May the words of my mouth and the meditation of my heart be acceptable in Thy sight, O Lord, my strength and my redeemer."

Easing back the warm covers, my feet meet the carpet. I slip on a pair of socks. My father taught me to make the bed, and I do so every morning. A made bed brings order, a sense of peace. I tuck and smooth the fitted sheet, the top sheet, the comforter. Pillows stand tall —two round, two gold, two lavender. I step back, satisfied.

With a small white remote, I click the diffuser. A mist of perfumed orange aroma fills the air. Another click—soft meditation music plays, caressing the room.

I unroll a yoga mat. With both feet together, I ease into the Sun Salutation, inhaling and exhaling into each posture. After four rounds, my body feels renewed, massaged from within and without.

This morning ritual grounds me. My bedroom remains sacred. No television. No distractions. Just me and the Creator.

At five feet three inches, I've maintained my weight and still wear a size four. As I scan the exterior of my uncovered body in the mirror, two six-inch scars stare back at me—each one a silent witness to my survival.

The upper scar is from an appendectomy in my late twenties. I remember the sharp, unrelenting pain when my daughter was only nine months old. A fleeting thought crossed my mind—an image of a childhood friend whose appendix had ruptured. That memory nudged me toward caution. At the time, I didn't attribute it to intuition or my inner self whispering a warning, but it was a touch of both. It saved my life.

After medical exams and tests, the doctor diagnosed me with appendicitis and called for immediate surgery. That incision, sculpted decades ago, became a symbol of life preserved.

The second scar, lower near my pelvic area, tells another story. In my late forties, my menstrual cycles grew erratic and heavy. My gynecologist discovered a fibroid—approximately the size of a six-month-old fetus—pressing against my organs. After much deliberation, a partial hysterectomy became the only viable option.

"Doctor, I want my ovaries saved," I said, my voice quivering. "They produce estrogen. Can you do that?"

"Yes," the doctor assured me with confidence.

The night before the procedure, I stood in the shower. Tears streamed down my face, blending with the water rushing from the showerhead. In hushed tones filled with grief, I spoke to my womb—my sacred center.

"Thank you, my womb, for bearing my children. You nurtured them until they were ready to live outside my body. Thank you. Thank you. Thank you."

I wept until I could weep no more. Then I laid in bed, praying harder than ever.

The surgery came and went. During recovery, my doctor showed me a photo of the fibroid. I stared briefly before letting the image fade from my mind. My thoughts turned to healing, to returning home, to fulfilling my responsibilities. The idea that I would never bear children again didn't devastate me. I had already released those tears. There were none left.

These physical scars from past joys and pain stir memories that live in my body. I think about mortality. One day, I will leave this world—but not today. Time is precious. Every minute is mine to honor.

As I walk from the bathroom, my eyes expand across the full scope of my bedroom, and I am pleased. The nine-drawer dresser, with its silver handles, stands like a mountain—majestic and unmoved. Above it, a wide mirror reflects not just my image but my journey.

Atop the dresser, glass and crystal awards glisten like trophies of resilience:

- IOTA Phi Lambda, Alpha Kappa Chapter: Outstanding Woman of the Year
- Alkebu-lan Academy: National Youth Service Award— Torchbearer to the Children of God. Doctor Monifa Imarogbe
- Winans Academy of Performing Arts: Five Years of Service – Doctor Shelley McIntosh
- IOTA Phi Lambda, Alpha Kappa Chapter: Igniting Our Business Connections – Observing I Honoree
- A glass nameplate: Doctor Shelley McIntosh, Principal

Two final pieces complete the display: a plaque and a certificate.

The plaque, from the University of Houston-Downtown, reads:

African American Faculty and Staff Image Award – Faculty Division

In honor of your contribution to the advancement of African American culture and history.

The certificate is from the Alkebu-lan Village Organization in Detroit:

Sheroes of the Diaspora: The Mary McLeod Bethune Education Award

Presented to Doctor Shelley McIntosh for embodying the principles of community, connectivity, and courage in education.

Next to this proud arrangement is my grandson Dwight Jr.'s graduation photo. It stands beside a black vase with gold overtones, overflowing with artificial long-stemmed violet flowers—both graceful and regal.

To the left of the dresser is a striking 48-by-35-inch painting by African American artist K.A. Williams. The image is of a Black woman in a white, sleeveless, full-length dress. Her back faces the viewer, but her presence commands attention. Chattel chains fall from her right wrist as her left hand lifts a jeweled crown to her head. She walks through a field of cotton toward freedom, stepping into her queendom. Beneath the image, the inscription reads: *"The first shall be last, and the last shall be first."* Each morning, this picture is one of the first things I see—and it continues to inspire me.

To the right of my bed is a crystal-based lamp, crowned with a white pleated shade. Slightly above it on the wall is a cherished collage of my daughter, Lateefah Dara. In the center, she is five years old, with a short-cropped Afro and fingers in her mouth, perched on her father's lap. To the left, an image of me holding her at nine months, dressed in a yellow snowsuit, her smile radiant. On the right, her graduation portrait from Michigan State University—capped, gowned, and glowing. These pictures tether me to the miracles of motherhood and the magic of memory.

Two large windows sit on the left side of the room, dressed in pastel gold drapes. Solid panels frame sheer ones, offering glimpses of tall pine trees outside. The soft natural light filters through, painting serenity across the room.

To the left of my bed is a black-rimmed desk with a stained-glass top and a three-tiered glass shelf. With its dark metal curves, it resembles a poised crane standing on one leg. Though purchased as a desk, it has been transformed into an altar.

Three tapered candles—red, black, and green—stand in tall glass holders at the center of the altar. They symbolize the cornerstone of my belief system. Red represents the blood Black people have shed, are shedding, and will continue to shed for freedom. Black signifies my racial identity—I am Black. I am African. Green embodies the promise and fertility of the Motherland. The redemption of Africa remains my ultimate dream, my forever idyllic idea.

My late husband, Fred McIntosh Jr., passed away two decades ago. His Bible lies open on the altar, its pages marked with yellow highlights of the scriptures he loved. My wedding ring rests upon them. I often reflect on the day we met, the moment we were engaged, and our wedding day. Though I miss him deeply, I feel mysteriously protected by his spirit.

To the left of his Bible is a framed 6-by-8-inch image of the Black Madonna and Child—a replica of the original painting at the Shrine of the Black Madonna in Detroit. Another depiction, this time carved in black wood, stands nearby. A glass crucifix, a pair of crystal angel wings, and a tulip plant complete the sacred arrangement.

Atop the mantel of the three-tiered shelf sits a small lamp. On the middle shelf are gifts from my daughter and friends: a ruby-colored pyramid, a miniature box of forever roses, an aromatic diffuser, and a striped porcelain elephant. On the lowest shelf rests my late husband's marble funerary urn, engraved with his name, birth date, and death date. Though his ashes have since been spread in Galveston, Texas, the urn remains a symbol of our enduring bond.

Beneath the altar are my late father's Johnston & Murphy size 13 brown shoes. They appear unworn—pristine, like much of his carefully maintained wardrobe. Every time my eyes fall on those shoes, I am reminded of his love, his strength, and his support. I am still comforted by his spirit—his invisible presence from a realm where the past blends seamlessly with the eternal now. My altar is a sanctuary that anchors me in the awareness of an ever-present, invisible God.

I believe my parents' spirits continue to guide and fortify me. According to an African belief, a person remains alive as long as their name is spoken. I know my parents live on—through their teachings and through me.

When I iron, it's because my mother taught me to press every part of a shirt with care. When I do laundry, it's because my father showed me how to separate light and dark clothes. When I exercise, it's because he instilled that habit early—teaching us jumping jacks and simple body movements like "head, shoulders, knees, and toes."

When I remind my son to pay his bills on time, I hear my father's voice echoing that same lesson. When I resist taking others' comments too personally, it's because my mother advised me to imagine wearing a yellow rubber raincoat—letting criticism slide off like rain. When I clean, it's because they taught me the discipline of a well-kept home: how to make a bed, scrub a bathroom, and mop a floor.

I'm convinced they live in me because of the way I live my life.

I view life as a continuum shared by angels, warriors, and ancestors. Many souls have crossed my path—each offering something vital. Some brought wisdom, others opened doors. Some made me laugh or offered friendship. Each one a gift.

I think often about the cycle of life: how birth brings a soul into this world, and death ushers them out. Many of my beloveds have transitioned:

- Bessie Craig and Annie Miller – my grandmothers
- John Miller (step-grandfather)
- Rufus and Ruth Miller – my parents
- Rufus James Miller, Jr. – my brother
- Vernice Miller – my eldest sister
- Unice Miller – Vernice's twin, who died at birth
- Robert Lee Craig, Leon Miller, George Miller, Eddie Cooper, Samuel Hinkle – my uncles
- Mary Cooper and Rose Hinkle – my aunts
- Fred McIntosh – my beloved husband
- Ni'jah Monifa Johnson – my granddaughter

Each of them is a warrior. An angel. Though gone, I do not feel alone.

11

AWAKENINGS

I remember how my youngest grandson, David, like an angel, delivered a message to me. He was just five years old when I taught him reading lessons in one of the beautifully lit meeting spaces at the Southfield Library. After about forty-five minutes, we packed up our books, workbooks, pencils, and paper to leave. As we exited through the automatic glass doors, I noticed the sky had darkened. A cool, slightly stronger breeze swept through the branches of the trees.

"David, it has gotten colder," I announced with authority.

"No, Nana, no," he replied.

"Yes, it has," I insisted, certain that Nana knew best.

"No, Nana, no," he repeated, unwavering in his stance.

"Yes, it has, David. Look at how the branches and leaves are swaying because of the wind," I pointed out, reinforcing my observation.

Then, in a soft and calming voice, he said,

"Aw, Nana, the trees are just waving at you."

His words quieted me. His perception sharpened mine. His way of seeing stroked my awareness. His confidence shifted my consciousness. From that moment on, the trees waving at me became a new reality. His simple message enlightened my soul.

My life has been filled with such messages—whispers that have freed my inner power. One in particular stands out as an awakening. Years ago, while sitting in a conference room at the University of Houston Main Campus, I experienced a profound shift.

There were eight of us, all professors of teacher education, gathered around an immense oblong wooden table. Our task was to organize a One-Day Student Teacher Professional Development workshop. Dr. Warner, the only male in attendance, chaired the meeting. He opened with an invitation for each of us to introduce ourselves.

Each female colleague shared a brief narrative—most focused more on being mothers or grandmothers than on their professional or academic achievements. I followed suit. Though I briefly mentioned that my life's work included developing children socially, emotionally, physically, spiritually, and academically, I offered no in-depth account of my professional journey.

Lastly, Dr. Warner introduced himself. His story was a litany of leadership—one position after another—culminating in his current role as Chair of the College of Education. I was impressed. And then it struck me like lightning: why didn't my female colleagues—or even I—include our professional accomplishments in our introductions?

That day, I awakened to a new self-awareness: I must see myself in totality. I must be brave enough to speak of my journey—of my victories, my sadness, and my joy.

As Dr. Warner closed his introduction, he turned toward me, looked directly into my eyes, and said with sincerity,

"You are a passionate, quiet warrior."

Perhaps he sensed it in my voice or read it in my expression. I dare not define the reason with certainty. But to this day, I believe he was right.

I am a Quiet Warrior.

ABOUT THE AUTHOR

Dr. Shelley McIntosh—Monifa Dara— holds a doctorate in Curriculum and Instruction from the University of Houston. She unequivocally states, "Education chose me."

Her studies and research center on the social, spiritual, and academic development of Black children; the spiritual voices of teachers; effective literacy instruction for African Americans; and biblical history. She is the author of numerous professional articles and six published books.

Her dedication to self-determination and the well-being of children is candidly expressed in *Mtoto House: Vision to Victory—Raising African American Children Communally*. In *Genesis II: The Re-Creation of Black People*, she presents a culmination of Black Liberation Theology lessons. *A Principal's Tale: Life in 31 Days* captures the personal and professional journey of an urban school principal, while its second edition, *A Principal's Tale: A Self-Determined Leader*, offers insights and resolutions to real challenges schools face.

Her memoir, *Memoir of a Black Christian Nationalist: Seeds of Liberation*, chronicles her spiritual and ideological journey as a member of the Shrines of the Black Madonna and explores the tenets developed by Reverend Albert B. Cleage, Jr., founder of both the Shrines and the theology of Black Liberation. Her latest work, *Warriors and Angels*, extends her memoir with a deeper focus on social, mental, and spiritual resilience.

Dr. McIntosh has served as bishop, cardinal, national youth director, professor of urban education, English Language Arts coach, teacher, and principal. She is the founder of **Child Focused Consulting Company, LLC** and the **Ni'jah Monifa Literacy Center.**

"So teach us to number our days, that we may apply our hearts unto wisdom."

—Psalm 90:12 (KJV)

📍 shelleymcintosh.com

CALL AND RESPONSES OF THE SHRINE OF THE BLACK MADONNA

Ritual for the Black Nation

Call: What time is it?

Response: It's Nation time!

Call: Nation time means there is nothing more sacred than the liberation of Black people.

Response: Then let the Black Nation rise!

Call: Nation time means the rejection of individualism.

Response: Then let the Black Nation rise!

Call: Nation time means total commitment to the Black Liberation struggle.

Response: Then let the Black Nation rise!

Call: Nation time means putting aside integration and loving our own Black selves.

Response: Then let the Black Nation rise!

Call: Nation time means Black Christian Nationalist time.

Response: Then let the Black Nation rise!

Call: BCN brings us together as one people. Umoja!

Response: Umoja, Umoja, Umoja!

Call: BCN leads the way to a Black communal society. Ujamaa!

Response: Ujamaa, Ujamaa, Ujamaa!

Call: BCN builds power for Black freedom, Uhuru!

Response: Uhuru, Uhuru, Uhuru!

Call: BCN is the answer, Umoja, Ujamaa, Uhuru!

Response: Umoja, Ujamaa, Uhuru means Unity, Program, and Freedom!

Call: We need Black brothers and sisters who give, work, and train to serve the Black Nation, Ujamaa!

Response: Ujamaa, Ujamaa, Ujamaa!

Call: We need Black brothers and sisters who are willing to die for the Black Nation, Uhuru!

Response: Uhuru, Uhuru, Uhuru!

Call: We remember Jesus, the Black Messiah, Nat Turner, Marcus Garvey, Brother Malcolm, and millions who died for Black liberation, Uhuru!

Response: Uhuru, Uhuru, Uhuru!

Call: Across the world which we once ruled as Black men and women, and to which we brought the gifts of civilization, religion, and science, we now stand powerless and enslaved, Uhuru!

Response: Uhuru, Uhuru, Uhuru!

Call: Though scattered and powerless, we are an African people. Let the Black Nation rise, Uhuru!

Response: Uhuru, Uhuru, Uhuru!

Call: We cannot be free until our Motherland Africa, and all Black people everywhere are free. Let the Black Nation rise! Uhuru!

Response: Uhuru, Uhuru, Uhuru!

Call: We reject identification with our oppressor and accept a new value system and lifestyle taught by the Pan African Orthodox Christian Church Let the Black Nation rise! Umoja, Ujamaa, Uhuru!

Response: Umoja, Ujamaa, Uhuru means unity, program, and freedom.

All: Let the Black Nation rise, Uhuru, Uhuru, Uhuru!

We Seek the Experience of God

Leader: Kutafuta means that we have entered the Sacred Circle and we seek the experience of God.

Response: We open ourselves to receive the power of God.

Leader: Kutamungu means that we can come upon God here where we are.

Response: If we seek, we will find.

Leader: When we are open, our inner divinity can be touched by the cosmic power of God and Kugasana will come like a mystical explosion.

Response: The overwhelming power of God enters into us, the Creative Intelligence of God directs us. We become one with God and with our people everywhere.

Leader: When our divinity comes into contact with the Higher Power, out of which it was created, we are born again in the fulness of life.

Response: The sacred triangles, the mystical sacraments, and the disciplines of the transforming community open us to receive the power of God.

Leader: In our surrender to God, Kujitoa, we have new strength for our earthly battles.

Response: We share a sacred trust with those who have gone before and with those who will come after. We are in total submission to the will of God. Kujitoa.

All: Kutafuta. Kutamungu. Kugasana. Kujitoa.

HYMNS

Go Tell It on the Mountain
Original: John Wesley Work, Jr. | Revised: BCN Choir

Chorus
Go, tell it on the mountain,
Over the hills and everywhere.
Go, tell it on the mountain
That the Black Messiah is born.

Verse
While shepherds kept their watching
O'er silent flocks by night,
Behold, throughout the heavens
There shone a Holy Light.

The Black Messiah
Jimmy Hightower-Okera

To this end were we born,
And for this cause we came into the world,
That we might bear witness to the truth.
Oh Lord!
We took a real good look at our minds,
And we know that it's Nation Time.

The Lord didn't call but a few
To build a Nation on Earth
And call it heavenly home.

Then they will know
Who the Black Messiah is—
Master of the Universe,
The Lord!

God Gave Me a Song
Ken Cole

God gave me a song
That Black people forever shall sing.
Freedom burns in my heart
Like a volcanic flame—
We shall be free.

My God has made no slave of me.
He gave me strength for unity,
To build a Nation Black and strong,
With power to fight and right the wrong.

With God on our side
And Jesus our Guide,
Our Nation Black shall rise again—
Once again!

Chorus
Power—the Black Nation shall rise.
Freedom—the Black Nation shall live.
Power! The Black Nation shall rise.
Freedom! The Black Nation shall live.
Power, freedom, power, freedom—
BCN for liberation.
Black Power!

We Decided to Make BCN Our Choice
Original: Dr. Alyn E. Waller | Revised: BCN Choir

Some folks would rather have houses and land,
Some folks choose silver and gold.
These things they treasure
And forget about their souls—
We've decided to make BCN our choice.

The road is rough,
The going gets tough,
And the hills are hard to climb.
We started out a long time ago—
There is no doubt in our minds—
We've decided to make BCN our choice!

Our God Is Black (Offertory Hymn)
Revised: BCN Choir

Our God is Black, and so are we.
For Him we struggle to be free—
To build a Nation here on Earth,
And find in life—not death—but worth.

POEMS BY REVEREND ALBERT B. CLEAGE, JR.

Transformation
The third Discipline

Transformation,
The third discipline,
Involves the healing journey within—
Whereby we free ourselves
From the protective shields and blocks
By which, in isolation,
We have sought to protect the ego
Which we have mistaken for our being.

We have lived lives of quiet desperation,
Locked in a prison house
Of loneliness.
Afraid to bring the guilt
Of our repressed lives
Up into consciousness.
Deliberately
Choosing emptiness

To avoid vulnerability to pain.

We sought to anesthetize our emotions
So that we could neither love nor hate,
Nor feel.
We were closed away
In a shell of our own making.
Neither the sunrise nor the sunset
Could fill us with awe.

Neither the oceans,
The mountains,
A baby's laugh,
Nor a scream of pain,
Could break through our defenses.
We were cut off from life
And experiences.
We were the walking dead.

Transformation
Has shown us a light
At the end of a long tunnel.
We can change—
If we but have the courage
To break down the walls of isolation
And open ourselves to the pain of **KUA**,
The pain of becoming who we already are.

Renunciation
The first Discipline

Renunciation,
The first discipline,
Demands conscious acts of confession,
Repentance, and penance.

I am strengthened for this task
By honest participation in the fellowship,
Rituals, encounters, and divine obligations
Of the "Group" to which I have been assigned.

Renunciation
Enables me to cast aside escapism in all its forms.
I renounce the acceptance of "Black inferiority,"
Which I have been taught
By the operant conditioning of white oppression.

I renounce the futile dream of integration,
Which wastes my energies
In vain efforts to create a "non-people."

I renounce the "slave culture,"
A subculture of the powerless
Which has become, for me, a fantasyland
In which I dream away my life.

I renounce all of these weaknesses
Which block the building of a Black Community—
A counter-culture with power.

I carefully define boundaries and erect barriers
To separate me
From the evil, insane world I have renounced.

Identification
The second Discipline

Identification,
The second discipline,
Touches the very core of my being,
Calling me back to my ancestral roots
In Africa—
Where the first man was created,
Black and beautiful,
In a lush garden of plenty.

We were a Chosen People,
Favored above all people—
Until we rebelled against God,
The cosmic power and creative intelligence
Out of which we have been created.

But we could not escape.
God remained incarnate within us.

Identification
Opens my eyes to the defilement
Of our enslavement
By a ruthless enemy
Who brutalizes and exploits
And declares us to be inferior.

I identify with my people everywhere,
Rejoicing in their triumphs,
And suffering their pain.
We are one.

I recoil from the brutal separation
Forced upon us.
The spiritual powers of my fathers
Engulf me.
The voice of the drums
Calls me back to the gods of my people,
And I join in their healing firelight dance
In the sacred circle beneath the stars.

Identification

Makes it possible for me to see the power of Jesus—
Before he became the captive
Of the church with its sterile white individualism,
With its futile effort to wipe out
The African foundations of Christianity.

Identification with my brothers and sisters
Brought me back to God.

LETTERS

Mama

By Italo

It took me a while to get my own style.
When I first left Houston, I thought
I'd get crazy and buck wild.
But what was I thinking?
I'm Monifa's child!

She raised me right,
Showed me the light,
Directed me on which way to go—
As if she was the wind and I was a kite.

She knew I wanted to have fun,
And that's why I left.
Moved to Atlanta all by myself.

My first two months were exciting, no doubt.

But as the weeks went on,
My smiles turned to pouts.
Because problems arose,
And I was unsure which way to go.

But I reflected on my Mama's teachings,
And I got back into the flow—
Into all the right directions,
If you know what I mean.

I understand now:
Life ain't all about ladies and green.
But it took me a while
To realize the style
My Mama gave me
Would be the one in the end
That saves me.

Hey Auntie

From Joy

I suspect that you have lots of mixed emotions this weekend. Here's what I want you to think about:

If your goal in participating in the Shrines of the Black Madonna was to liberate Black people, then your efforts have proven fruitful. Your time, sacrifices, tears, energy, and intelligence have liberated every person by any of the aforementioned attributes you have graced—some for a day, some for a week, some for years, and for many, a lifetime.

This is my opinion on your effect on adults. You may have liberated them from a slave mentality, low self-esteem, selfishness, individualism, or even an unhealthy physical lifestyle.

As for the children you've worked tirelessly for—do you not see that your words, your classes, your research, your spiritual gifts are the reason why each and every one of us are capable of doing what we do?

The way we are able to comprehend and read and write well, our ability to compete in the world with confidence, learning to type, discernment to navigate the illusions of this country— these things and many more have liberated us in ways you have seen and some you will never know.

There are hundreds of Black people who would have fallen prey to the ills of society had it not been for you and all that you encompass and so freely shared with your people. Is that not liberation?

Did you think you were going to save millions? Did you put a quota on it? You have reached your goal over and over again, if indeed that goal was to dedicate your life to the liberation of Black people.

It is continued in the way we speak to our loved ones. It is continued in the way we interact at work. It is continued when we are able to have open communication with the Creator— because you taught us that.

You taught us yoga to open our bodies to discover our divinity.

YOU HAVE LIBERATED US SO THAT WE MAY KNOW THAT WE ARE DIVINE. THAT IS PRICELESS.

I have come to see that we have many lives in this one human experience. Your work during that phase of your life is done. And you did it well.

Give yourself credit. The universe needed that when you gave it.

Doubt cannot survive here, so please stop feeding it.

I love you and I appreciate you. Now go and enjoy this phase of your life!

Freedom burns in your heart like a volcanic flame.
We shall be free.
God has made no slave of you.
Free yourself now.
Make peace with what you have done—
For it was never, and will never be, in vain.

My Letter to the Children of the Shrines of the Black Madonna

"Children are a gift from the Lord; they are a reward from Him."
"Jesus said, 'Let the little children come to me, and do not hinder them, for the kingdom of heaven belongs to such as these.'"
"Children's children are a crown to the aged, and parents are the pride of their children."

Dear Children of Alkebu-lan,

I am spiritually compelled to write this letter to all of you. Notice that I titled it *The Blessings of Mothers*. We will not be with you always on the physical plane. This is the very reason I want to take this time to bestow blessings upon you—

blessings from me and all those Nation Mothers who committed their lives for your benefit.

As children, your memories and experiences in Alkebu-lan may differ—and they should. Some experiences were joyful, while others may have left you feeling abandoned by your parents. As your Nation Mothers, our journey was one of commitment, sacrifice, and love.

In the 1970s, we were young, in our twenties. As nature would have it, we started our families and became young mothers. Many of us quit our full-time jobs to become full-time Nation Builders. This was our decision, because we believed we could build a better world for you—a sanctuary, a home, a self-sustaining Nation.

So, we cared for you collectively. Before there was a formal nursery, each group of adults took responsibility for feeding, supervising, and teaching the small children of their group.

Formal institutions were developed: Alkebu-lan Academy, Alkebu-lan Nursery, and Mtoto House. Childcare evolved into institutional structure. Young mothers organized schedules, purchased food, prepared meals, developed academic programs, washed and ironed uniforms, cleaned Mtoto houses, walked or drove you to school, supervised communal showers, and taught you African history. We taught you to read before kindergarten, provided afterschool tutoring, and led you in group meetings and devotionals.

Our goal was to raise children who were better than we were.
We did it all for our children, Nation children, Africa's children.

Now, your Nation Mothers are in their 70s and 80s. Our once black hair is speckled with gray—or all gray. There are more years behind us than in front of us.

At the same time, many of you are in your fifties or quickly approaching it. You have become doctors, lawyers, engineers, nurses, teachers, coaches, entrepreneurs, social workers, skilled tradesmen, entertainers, administrators, artists, professors, pastors, parents, and grandparents.

You are the prayers and dreams of Nation Mothers!

Generations of Alkebu-lan span the 1970s, 1980s, 1990s, and 2000s. You are in Detroit, Atlanta, Houston, Maryland, Tanzania, and places I may not even know. Sadly, many of you don't know each other. You are a mighty force—an educated and skilled community, with knowledge and shared experiences, but disconnected.

The gift of power is within your reach.

We Nation Mothers are with you now—but in time, we will disappear.

My wish is that you commit yourselves to connecting all generations of Alkebu-lan—over 2,000 of you.
Recognize your power.
Unify.

FAMILY PHOTOS

Parents' Wedding

Mother Ruth Lee Miller

Father Rev Rufus James Miller

Child Focused Team

Granddaughter Ni'jah Monifa

Grandson David

Grandson Italo, Son Italo

Grandson Italo

Grandson Dwight Jr.

Daughter Lateefah, Dad David

Siblings - Vernice, Rufus, Jackie

Sister Jackie; Nieces - Jakneka and Joy; Great Nieces - Jziah, Jade, and Jasir

Grandson Saddiq

Baby Shelley